A BOOK TO FIND YOUR SOUL

by

CONSTANTINA ANTONOPOULOS

off the top of
my head,
from the bottom of
my heart

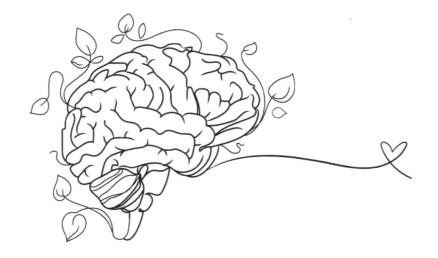

Published by:
Maudlin Pond Press, LLC
PO Box 53, Tybee Island, Georgia 31328, USA

ISBN: 978-1-959563-33-4

To my dear children: Peter and Noel,

<u>*Off the top of my head, from the bottom of my heart*</u> is dedicated to the both of you. You are my constant inspiration, my source of joy, and the reason I continue to reach for the stars. Your love, curiosity, and laughter are woven into every page. You both helped me through all my adversities and taught me patience and purpose. Thank you! May you always chase your dreams, think freely, and know that no matter where life takes you, you carry my heart with you.

With all my love, your mom,

Constantina Antonopoulos

The Secret Sauce.

How do you do the same thing that others do, but differently?

My beautiful Grandma Athena taught me how to make Greek coffee. Although it is not difficult, my Mom still cannot make it as good as I can, sorry Mom. That is all thanks to my Grandma! I paid attention and my Grandma taught me when to take it off the stove top, at just the right time, and how to pour it to ensure it has the right amount of foam on the top so it does not look flat. In that lesson, my Grandma taught me a very important mindset. The reason why I learned that lesson, and it has stayed with me until this day, is my Grandma taught me how to make Greek coffee with LOVE. That was her secret sauce.

Everything in life requires a secret sauce.

What's yours?

Reflecting back on my Grandma's coffee technique, I can see how in life we have to follow directions, instructions and put in the right ingredients to get the ultimate end result. That can be for a meal you prepare, consistency in training, building relationships and reaching goals in your career and life. What's your take on how you approach something? How can you jazz it up and make it your own?

The secret sauce, if you will, can be dedication, love, respect – fill in the blanks. Whatever works for you, do it! Be bold!

The bottom line is, don't hold yourself back from using your special technique, perspective or unique way of pursuing your soul purpose! Ask yourself how you can do something differently, that others do the same? Put your twist on it!

Go for it!

Do not let fear deter you. Be different.

Be unique.

Nourish your soul.

Life is meant to challenge you.

Get out of your comfort zone. Work on healing yourself from past traumas that have hindered your growth.

We all have hurts and disappointments. Use them as your fuel to start the fire in your soul again.

Wake up the warrior in you! Be your own person!

Embrace the journey and all the lessons, they are your friends. Let them lead you to your abundance.

You have all the tools inside you.

Sharpen your mindset.

Strengthen your body.

Protect your soul.

Breathe!

You got this!

Mindset over Motivation.

Motivation is a quick fix.

Motivation is temporary.

Motivation needs constant deposits.

You set yourself up to fail when you rely on motivation because it's like an addiction that keeps you trapped and impaired. It's never enough.

Mindset is a way of life.

Mindset is a lifestyle that enables your mind to help you create your life, actively, proactively and with purpose.

Mindset is a way of life, that works for YOU, custom built for YOU!

Intentionally say you're going to do better and take action today. Let's go!

Forget the past. It's old.

Don't look at the future, it's too far away.

Ground yourself in the present.

It's NOW!

Start now!

Your mindset will navigate you out of the darkness and to your destination. You are in charge of picking where you want to go, who's going with you and what you want to pack.

That excess baggage from the past, throw it in the trash!

Are you all packed?

Good!

Get in your car, tap in where you want to go and follow the navigation system to YOUR life, YOUR way!

It's your life!

It's your highway!

I'm excited for you!

Send me postcards!

How much do you respect yourself?

Real question. Do you allow others to push your boundaries because you do not want to lose a friend, family member or a significant other?

People will value you when you respect yourself enough to stand up for who you truly are. Decide who you are and show up that way in every situation without bending your rules.

There isn't anything worse than losing yourself to make someone else happy, that you'll never make happy.

Read that again.

You have to protect your energy and stay true to who you are by respecting your boundaries and standards at ALL COSTS!

If you are not given the same energy back, as you give out, it's time to step back to yourself.

You owe it to yourself to remain true.

There is only one YOU!

You are priceless!

It is so important to stay present!

Your past should only allow you the opportunity to learn and grow from it. Don't dwell in it. You no longer live there.

Your future is determined by how well you learn and grow from your past, ONLY, if you can bring yourself to be in the present moment. Once you master that, you can maximize all you want for your future, with thought out actions that come to life.

Depression stems from the past and anxiety is built up for the future. You heal when you ground yourself and bring yourself in the moment of the PRESENT.

Breathe and look around you.

You're golden!

Life is beautiful!

How precious a gift the present is?

Cherish it!

Use the present to your advantage because it centers you and allows your mind, body and soul an opportunity to process, release and heal.

How are you staying in the present today?

New day, let's try this again.

The beauty in a new day is that you have yet another opportunity to change your life. How you ask? Start with your mindset.

The past is over. Use it as a reference, your own personal google search. The future has so many possibilities, ONLY if YOU start where you are, THE PRESENT.

The time is now! Start today! Think what you want to be in your life and act on it with every breath and step you take.

You want to strengthen your mind – read, pray and meditate. Listen to learn and stop overreacting and over responding! You want to get in shape – nourish your body, strength train, do cardio and stretch, while you breathe.

Yes, breathe!

It helps!

You want to feel grounded and connected – let's meditate again!

Quiet your mind from the noise of the world so you can hear what your mind, body and soul needs. It's that simple!

Be fearless! Go get this!

Today is YOUR DAY!

Trust in yourself.

When you believe and trust in yourself, you hold the power. That power builds your value and worth, not only for others, more importantly for yourself.

You know who you are on the inside. You know what you want and need. Why are you questioning yourself and allowing others to steer you in the way that they want you to go in?

Find the mental strength to follow through on what you want to do in your life. Take advice and opinions from others, as a reference point. Come back to yourself and ask yourself if that works for you, and if it doesn't, continue following your path.

Your life and your journey are yours, like your fingerprints are!

Why are you stopping yourself from reaching your full potential, based on what others think you should do?

Living in regret and what if, is more dangerous for your mindset than failing.

Failing is a stepping stone to success.

Regret is a life sentence of mindset stagnancy.

Don't allow that for yourself!

I am a big advocate for stressing the importance of balancing your mind, body and soul.

If you do not work on your internal well-being, your external will fall out of alignment. You are not going anywhere.

Nowadays, it is even more important to focus on your mental well-being. We are overly stimulated with social media, news and opinions of others. All that can hinder your progress and your health!

Fitness has always been in the spotlight. If you do not get your mindset right, your fitness will suffer. You have to be in the mindset where your mind and body communicate and work together. Mental focus in the gym is crucial. Proper nutrition and hydration is essential. The two have to go hand in hand.

Now let us talk my language – your soul. Yeah, that is right, your soul.

Work on it daily. Balance your chakras. Silence your mind with nature, prayer and meditation.

Be a good person.

Follow the golden rule. Love more! Give more! Help others win!

Once you master aligning your mind, body and soul, I guarantee you, you will reap the benefits in your life.

Let us raise the vibration of the world together, one person at a time.

Kindness is a relative of love. The two work hand in hand.

Kindness and love, if spread properly, are magnetic beams of energy that emit in ways that are magical. When you combine the two, they are quite a powerful duo.

Humans, animals and nature work well because of that duo.

Humans who use kindness and love as the foundation of anything they do have a greater chance of success. When you do things from a place of kindness and love, life feels better.

Life works better!

Life tastes better!

Animals portray their kindness and love without even having to use words. Think about that! That's wild! They show their kindness and love through their actions. A dog lays by its owner and the owner feels the kindness and love without anything being said. It's a heartwarming sense that heals!

The sun and the rain show their kindness and love to flowers by helping them grow. Nature helps animals in ways that should amaze you. That's faith! Animals, trees and flowers, trust Mother Nature to provide for them with her kindness and love! It's not even a discussion.

It just happens!

As humans we should look at nature and animals to understand that the flow of life is based on a trust system that is innately in all of us. It's that simple. It's that easy. Do things with kindness and love.

Period.

Will you run your day with kindness and love?

Let's talk about your heart.

Your heart feels things through even though your mind might tell you otherwise. I'm sure a lot of you have fallen in love with someone and truly lived through the statement: "love is blind."

Let's give your mind a rest for this one and focus on your heart......

Your heart beats inside of you to keep you alive. It's the center of everything. Your heart grounds and excites you in a different way than your mind does. Your mind often talks you out of things, while your heart is telling you to follow it. That's exhilarating!!!

Have you followed your heart? Are you following your heart?

When your heart is open, you allow life to happen for you. An open heart will allow love through. An open heart is a happy heart, which leads you to live a fulfilled and abundant life.

Mind, body and soul are an important trio. Your heart is equally as important as it plays the role of hydrating and pumping excitement, life and new meaning to that trio. Your heart adds zest to your life. Your heart also plays a significant role in your happiness because LOVE is the key. Love opens up all the windows and doors!

Usually your why in life has to do with your heart and love.

Allow your heart to beat with excitement today, and I encourage you all to use the phrase: "I Love You" as often as you can!

It makes a difference for your mind, body and soul health!

The focus should be on yourself and your life, no excuses!

If you are comparing your life to someone else's life, you are losing yourself in the process. Read that again.

When you focus on who you are and what you want for yourself and your life, the energy is magnetized and you will attract what you seek.

Make clear intentional goals for yourself and habitually follow through on them daily. One day, you will look around and you WILL be living the life you focused on building.

Think, believe, say it and act on it!

What does peace of mind mean to you?

As we mature, grow wiser and outgrow situations and people, we often realize that peace is a healthy and wealthy mindset to strive for.

You will never take off in your life, when you allow low vibrational people to hold you down.

When you are true to yourself and at peace with who you are and KNOW where you want to go, my advice is TO GO! Take off!

In order to grow, you have to trim the fat and utilize the knowledge that will get you to level up in your life. You know what you have to do. Take action and do it! Period.

An airplane takes off, regardless of anyone missing the flight. Don't miss your flight!

Managing your time properly is instrumental to your overall well-being.

When you allocate time with intention to strategically do certain things in order to attain your goals, you have mastered mindset.

Mindset is the balancing beam to your mental, physical, emotional and psychological health.

Wasting time today with excuses, will maximize temporary gratification, with the inevitable risk of minimizing success in the future.

"Still water runs deep" ~ Eileen Goudge

Maturity is silent
Be silent
Silence is wisdom
Be wise
Wisdom leads to greatness
Be great

Greatness unleashes your full potential and drives you to your purpose.

Less words, more action!

When you know who you are, you don't have to talk your way out of anything, or through anything.

It just flows!

A calm mind WILL win the war in advance.

It is crucial to clear your mind of negative thoughts, impulsive reactions and responses that compromise your leverage in a situation.

Move in silence and confidence.

Be strategic and stay on your path, regardless of the bumps on the road. Expect them, don't let them deter you.

When you find yourself fighting a war that has endless battles, your best ammunition is your mindset.

Strengthen your mindset, by balancing your emotions. You can feel through it. Don't act on it.

You're in this to WIN!

A day has 24 hours in it! You have time to do it all!

If you allocate your time properly, you can accomplish a lot.
It's a MINDSET GAME.

Get organized. Tap in the destination and stay in your lane.

What you focus on becomes your life. Read that again.

If someone doesn't have time for you, it's time to eliminate that person from your life and continue on your journey.

Stop allowing others to waste your time.

Stay in alignment with your life purpose by navigating your goals with intentional actions.

How does not staying in your lane affect your life?

I am a huge fan of discipline, purpose, persistence and direction. Those are a few key elements to ensuring you are on the right path in your life. Sometimes, the path you are on is not necessarily carved out. The roads may be bumpy. There may not be any road signs or exits, however if that's the road you have to navigate through to reach your destination, I urge you to stay in your lane because that is where you will find your purpose. You're afraid, that's okay, that will sharpen your senses to pay attention! This journey should excite you! This is where you feel alive and driven to help yourself and others as well!

It is my belief that it is crucial to know where one is headed. How? Speak it! Write it! Initiate the plan and follow through! It is possible to envision that when you push through the what-ifs you see yourself in the final destination. Don't allow the fear or the noise of others to distract you. If you believe it can be done, God (Destiny, the Universe, the Great Spirit) finds a way to help you through it. Anything is possible when you believe. Failing is not an option, it is simply a redirection to continue staying in your lane when you go off course.

Think of it this way, when we have somewhere to go, we tap in the address on our navigation system and follow the directions to get to where we are headed. We have to initiate an executed plan in order to get to our destination. It is the same way of thinking in our personal lives and with our careers.

Stay in your purpose!

Stay in your lane!

Believe me, I know it is so easy to get distracted nowadays. We all have many responsibilities that may overwhelm us to the degree that we justify our excuses of why we are not disciplined in our purpose. My advice, when that happens is to think of yourself driving in your car to a destination. If you look in the rear-view mirror all the time, you can crash. If you decide to exit another way, you may find yourself off your life path. You have to drive forward and put your energy towards getting to where you are meant to be your best self.

We are allowed to fumble.

Just readjust and stay in your lane to get to where your soul is meant to be.

On the other side of the door is a new beginning – walk through it.

We have all had disappointments in life. Things that don't go as we planned, set-backs, rejections and plain and simply put, painful events. All those heartbreaking, life-changing events usually happen at our weakest moments, and when we are almost at the finish line. That is usually when the enemy tries to distract you and messes with your mind. Shield yourself with prayer and the Word of God. "No weapon formed against thee shall prosper" Isaiah 54:17, my favorite verse in the Bible. Realign your mindset to push through the negative and watch what happens in your life.

Almost there? Yes, if you can imagine your life as a series of closed and open doors, you can understand how life works. How we respond and react to situations makes all the difference, in regard to things being delayed, or transforming in our lives.

We are all guilty of standing in front of a closed door, knocking on it, trying to break it down. Those experiences may have come through work, a relationship, or even on our own personal and spiritual growth. At those times, God, the Universe, Divine, whatever you may believe in, steps in and either shuts that door down or pushes you in another direction.

That open door is what we were manifesting and or wishing for, for a long time. However, sometimes we stand in our own way, inside our thoughts, revisiting past traumas and events in our minds. What if that, and what if this? At that time, we have to allow healing, self-care and meditation, all tools that help immensely. Give yourself time to do the work and you will find yourself walking through that door and being amazed with the better version of yourself, on the other side.

Whatever stage you are in your life, know one thing – all that is meant for you, will find you. Don't be hard on yourself when you feel stuck. The day you feel stuck the most may be the last day before you walk through the door to your new beginning.

Your new life is one thought away. Get yourself in the right mindset.

The road to greatness leads to a magical place perceived in your strong mindset.

All is possible when you hit that benchmark.

However the journey is lonely, difficult and definitely will kick your ass.

Challenge yourself. You'll be grateful when you do!

At times you will want to give up. Don't!

In order to achieve greatness you need to do the work that's required. Do it!

Heal your inner child.

Do the necessary shadow work to address the emotions that lurk in the depths of your subconscious and your soul.

Face it all head on!
Face yourself!
Face your fears!

And know you are at the right place and on the right path to get to your greatness.

You have planted the seeds
You earned it!
Go get it!
It's yours!

Use the rear-view mirror as your benchmark.

Did you ever get into your car and leave a place and keep on looking in the rear-view mirror? Sometimes you reminisce. Other times you feel nostalgic. And often times, you just want to depart from that location as fast as you can.

Life is a vehicle that transports us through different seasons, places, ages and phases. We have to be mindful and place a rear-view mirror in our mind's eye to remind, guide and help us realize lessons learned, to move forward.

Quite often, we obsessively focus in that rear-view mirror to the point that we may miss what is in front of us. We live a "move on," "move forward" life. The reverse feature should only be used if you have to maneuver your life, like a vehicle, to get out of a place that you find yourself stuck in.

Utilize the rear-view mirror as your compass to guide you, through lessons and experiences learned, to your next destination, leveling up.

Your next destination will lead you to your transformation, elevation and give you the ability to become an elite driver, both behind the wheel and in your life.

Be patient as you navigate through the next phase. Focus on the road in front of you, with the confidence that you are becoming your purpose. On occasion, look in the rear-view mirror and acknowledge your accolades in life.

Be kind to yourself and affirm all you have accomplished.

Take a deep breath and keep pushing through.

Safe driving and remember to always... Nourish your soul.

If you were blessed to wake up today, you have an opportunity to start fresh.

Yesterday is not only gone, but it sets you in a position to win or reassess what made you fail to do better today. Use that knowledge, those feelings of regret or fear, to push through and fight for your life purpose. Shine through it!

You can do it. Change how you perceive a situation. Change your approach and you may be surprised when you find all the enlightenment needed was to start with a winning approach. Execute that idea to attain your goals. You are in control of your mind. Train your mind to love who you are!

We all have different journeys. There are many ways to do something. Do what feels right for you. Your soul will tell you. That gut feeling, tune into that.

That's your soul, working with your inner child to unveil the real you.

This should be exhilarating because with this new day, new attitude and new perspective, you will feel energized, powerful and grounded.

Welcome failures because they are blessings in disguise. Failures build the foundation in ways we may not initially process what is happening. However, in hindsight, you will find it all happened how it was supposed to.

What broke you, will end up being a part of the ingredient needed to make you, YOU.

Trust yourself.

Trust the process.

Reintroduce your inner child to your soul.

We all have heard the statement: "From the mouths of babes." A child is so pure, innocent and carefree. A child uses their imagination to create. When we lose that gift, we drift off of our soul purpose path.

As we are growing up, most of us cannot wait to become an adult. What we have difficulty understanding as young children, is that when that happens, there may be a disconnect between our inner child and our soul. Most of us struggle with that disconnect, disassociation and desensitization for many years, not knowing what we have to do to get back to that inner child and soul connection. That inner child allowed us to see the world with infinite possibilities. When we let go of that inner child, we lose ourselves. Often times, that's what we are searching for as adults, to reconnect to our inner child with our soul, and integrate that into our lives. We can reconnect with our inner child when we allow healing to take place through authentic self-reflection, meditation and believing in yourself. And once you tap into all that, it's a game changer!

I lost myself to find my soul, many times during this journey that began 12 years ago for me.

I'm hoping to help people come back to life from all the past few years' effect on our mental health, through support, inspiration and faith, based off of my personal life experiences.

Mindset is key!

We have to reframe our mind to allow us to excel.

Once you connect your inner child with your soul, you will go places that your mind and body could never take you to alone. The inner child, soul, mind and body collaborating as a solid unit is what we should all aim for.

We are all connected energetically.

When we open up our mind's eye and truly make an energetic connection with someone, it initially starts with a thought. That thought then connects to our heart and comes out as passion, through our soul.

Our eyes will grab our attention.
Our minds connect with a thought that leads to a feeling transmitted through our heart and soul. It's pure, magnetic magic after that point.

Through our souls, we exude a magnetic and energetic chain reaction that connects us all together in both negative and positive ways. Let us all strive to thrive in a positive way!

As Derick Grant, DG Mindset says: "As you believe in your mind, so you will be in your life....the energy of someone who controls their life from inside out...."
Everything starts from within our minds, hearts and souls. When we all connect our positive energies together, that reaction can move mountains.

Mindset Check.

Hey you! Excuse me for interrupting your negative thoughts. I encourage you to be mindful of your thoughts and how you talk to yourself today.

Spring clean your subconscious and start organizing your thoughts to reach your greatness. You can do this!

Put your right foot on the path to your higher self. Choose the colors and scenery you want around you to ignite the power within you to make this journey your own.

You have the tools you need to use your mindset to write your next chapter of your life.

Will it be easy? No! Will it be worth it? YES!

Ask yourself what are you willing to sacrifice with the choices you make?

We all have an opportunity to start fresh every day. We can choose to follow the crowd, stay stagnant, or choose to speak up for what we believe in. The choices we make WILL affect a lot of people in our lives. Choose wisely. Think things through.

Every choice we make can be a positive, or a negative. Every choice we make can sacrifice a huge part of our life, and other lives, without us even being aware at the time. Be smart!

Be proactive with your mindset. See far ahead and be mindful of the choices you make because those choices may impact the people you love in the future, to a degree that is very dangerous for their wellbeing, like our children.

Doing something is a decision. Not doing something is a decision. Following the crowd is a decision. Following your gut is a decision.

Can one person change the world? No! Can we all do our part to change the world together? Yes! Or are you being distracted in a way where you can't see the clear picture ahead?

Make your choices based on the wellbeing of those you love, today and for the future. Don't get distracted.

Manners, Morals and Integrity ~ great ingredients for authenticity.

We all strive every day to become the best version of ourselves. We grind and hustle to be on top of our game. We post content to get likes and to prove our worth and what value we bring to the table. We compete with the world that honestly sets such high standards, and at times, impossibilities to be able to attain that perfection, that is often times, an illusion.

Is there such a thing as perfection? The perfect life, spouse, children, house, car? How do we as individuals measure perfection against what others tell us it should be? That is setting us up for failure. Think about the pressure that we put on ourselves, approaching life through the eyes of others. We should do life our way! Be different! Be you!

What we should be focusing on is our growth as individuals. We all have a uniqueness to bring into the world. Bring it! Show the world who you are.

Everything starts from within. You have to be comfortable enough with the reflection looking back at you in the mirror. You have to be comfortable enough with yourself when you are alone, to actually love who you are, in public and on social media.

Are you the same person everywhere? Or are you wearing masks to attract attention to give you temporary gratification, in different settings?

If you work on your manners, morals and your integrity, at all times, that's when you are your true self. Be honest with yourself. Hold yourself accountable. Do the work to heal the traumas and insecurities. Be mindful of your thoughts, words and actions. The time invested in this will reap huge benefits in your life. Then go out there and help others. That is an authentic life, filled with purpose and focus.

Go into the world as yourself, not your mask(s)! Be kind. Be mindful. Give back. Be selfishly selfless!

There are no coincidences in life.

Life is filled with synchronicities.

We are all energetically connected.

Once we are aware of that, it's a game changer.

The shift begins, where you can attain the reality that you want to live in, by using your mind as a magnet.

Think through it, to get to it!

You're the author of your life.

Ask and you shall receive.

Intentional thoughts, with a vision and fueled by purpose, are magnetic!

Use the power of your thoughts to manifest your future. Add to that your soul purpose, and boom, energetically you are there.

The power lies within you.

Do things happen to you, or FOR you?

I believe this question can be answered differently at various stages in your life. It also depends on what the situation is that you are facing. The bottom line is, are you going to choose to you, or for you?

Personally, I have experienced both ends of the spectrum. The mindset of things happening to you and not for you, was one that I carried into my adult life, until a few years ago. I'm so grateful to have experienced both sides because it led me to my deeper understanding of what is truly important in life. The gift for me was the ability to help others see the light at the end of the tunnel because I too experienced the darkness. There is hope! Change your perspective. Change your mindset. Change your life.

We have the ability to choose how we react and respond to a situation. Often times, we are programmed in accordance to what we have been exposed to through our childhood. Unfortunately, if we have traumas and insecurities that we bring into adulthood from childhood, we continue those patterns that make life more difficult. The good news is you can change that mindset. It takes a lot of work, but it can be done. It starts with you! Baby steps. Start now!

If you are of the mindset that things happen to you, as I did in the past, you limit yourself for growth. The negative reaction and perspective puts your mind, body and soul in lockdown mode. If that's your approach, mindfully switch one word, "for..."

Once you switch that one word, and you are of the mindset that things are happening for you, your life changes. You open all the windows, doors and opportunities for your abundance. Your vibration rises and your blessings become limitless. You allow lessons to be learned and you give yourself the ability to try different approaches to solve problems.

Take each setback as an opportunity to pause and see the bigger picture. When you realize things are working out for you, the way they should, and your mindset is: "All things are happening for me," your life will flow and you will have the ability to reassess what truly works for your higher good.

Today is the perfect day to start that mindset!

Who Are You?

No, seriously, who are you? Do you even remember who you are, or who you were meant to be?

We are all born to be ourselves, not to copy others. However, we are molded by our parents, our teachers, our friends, or we are limited by our weak mindset. When you add trauma, self-doubt and fear to that, you're entering the danger zone.

Hold on, there's hope, you can reactivate that part of your soul when you realize you are living in hamster mode. Accept and reset. Heal yourself! Why are you limiting your life? The only one stopping you is you. Get out of your head! I urge you to do the work to get yourself back, mind, body and soul. You will thank me!

It's time to spring clean your mindset. It's time to close that door to a relationship that was toxic. It's time to nurture and nourish your soul so you can get out of feeling that brain fog that won't let the sun in. Open the shades in your mind and let the light in!

You were made to thrive, not survive. You were made to live abundantly. That thing, in the middle of your chest, should beat with excitement and align with your mind to revive your soul. When that happens, there's no stopping you.

Staying Real in a Fake World.

How difficult is it to hear yourself think? There are so many distractions and out-side noises that cause interference within ourselves. Be intentional with making time to quiet the noise so you can listen to yourself!

Have you ever stopped to truly listen to who you are and what you want to do, without being misled by others' thoughts and opinions of you?

The beauty of soul searching lies within the pain and hard work it takes to find yourself again. This life journey always brings you back to connecting your inner child with your soul.

The disconnect happens for a reason.....

We all have experienced a disconnect from our true selves. Life has a way of bringing you back with experiences and lessons, along your journey. Embrace all the challenges, for they are your friend!

When we can see the world through the eyes of our inner child and we can show up with our soul ignited, is when we step into greatness and live our life with soul purpose.

We are all here to make a difference. We are all important in the bigger picture of life. We all serve a purpose and it is our obligation to do the inner work to become #shiftchangers.

Be authentically yourself. Show your true colors and don't dim your light to fit in.

Shine bright!

There are so many ways to get to your destination.

Do you ever stop and look around you and truly take in how wondrous the world is!

Or are you stuck in your stagnant mindset that limits your true potential?

We all have 24 hours in the day. When it's sunny, cloudy, snowing or raining, we all experience that as well. How are you utilizing the time you have each day? How are you perceiving the weather – is it affecting your mood? Be true to yourself and I give you permission to kick your own butt and get the f up and change your mindset to change your life! Get up! Let's go!

Your mind has the ability to take you to places and make you feel like you have superpowers. Your mind can also stop you in your tracks. Don't allow that! Take each day and allocate time for your responsibilities, yourself and the steps needed to cross that bridge. Don't say you'll cross that bridge when you get to it. What are you doing to prepare yourself for that day? Put in the work now!

When you get to that bridge, and your mindset is strong, if you're not able to cross it, you'll find another way to get to your vision. Where there's a will, there's a way!

Bottom line is, you can't get to what you want tomorrow, if you're not preparing for it today.

Let the past offer you the foundational materials needed to build your path with momentum in the present, creating endless possibilities with several ways to get to your destination.

Let's get down to the nitty gritty.

We are all different versions of ourselves, at different times of our lives. That is the beauty of living an authentic life, you get to decide what you need to work on and how you want to show up in the world. Every day is a new beginning!

I wear many hats. I have always been a single mom, even when I was married! I grew up with my two children and I was their mom, chauffeur, tutor, chef, doctor and at times their police officer. You need to have your sh!# together if you are to take full responsibility of other humans. You are obligated to ensure they grow up to be well functioning adults who can contribute in positive ways in the world.

A lot of pressure, but day by day, mindfully and with Grace and Acceptance, it can be done! If I can, you can!

I'm on here as a Mindset Coach, not because I think I'm better than anyone else, or because I know more. I feel more. I feel for people's pain and all they are up against. It isn't easy being a human.

Wow, when I got that memo, I was like wait, what? I have to do all that?

But we do it! And I encourage all of you to do it with Grace. Be patient with yourself and at what stage you are at in your life. I know it is difficult when you are on social media and you see everyone living a life that you think you want and is perfect. No one leads a perfect life. I don't! I have been through it and I'm a work in progress. I'm healing, while I'm helping others heal as well!
Love the life you live!

Where you stand right now – that's YOU – only one of YOU. Be kind to yourself with your words and thoughts because YOU were made to be amazing!

At the end of the day, you have to answer to yourself.

Living a fulfilling life comes with a lot of hard work. You have to show up every day as your best version. If you feel you aren't your best version, start diving into areas of your life that need attention. With dedicated effort, a plan and consistency, you will find you're redirecting yourself to infinite possibilities.

Remind yourself this is not a competition with others. You set the pace and standards for your life but START somewhere! START NOW!

We are never ready. We are never the finished product. You have to decide that you are the director of your movie and lead the way to your best life. This should excite you because you are creating your life. Creation eliminates stagnation. Life is creation! Live your life!

Adulthood is often when we realize all we learned, we have to unlearn. We manually need to assess our minds and pick what serves us and discard what doesn't. Tough work! It can be done! Get your confidence back by tackling your fears!

At times this can be painful and difficult to do. The truth usually is a big wake up call. Set your alarm clock!

How willing are you to look in the mirror and admit to yourself that regardless of the flaws, the mistakes and the adversities, that you will quiet out the noise of the past, bring yourself to the present and utilize both experiences, for a future that defines you? Let's go!

Redefine yourself.

Be courageous enough to work on yourself!

I assure you, once you take the first step, you'll realize that you are exactly where you need to be.

The resources are within you. The success is within you.

Find it!!

GRATEFUL.

I am turning 54 tomorrow! I say that with such gratitude because I am fortunate and blessed with several gifts from God. I made it through some ridiculous battles and I *effen* got through it! That's because God has instilled things in me that I utilized to make it through and I am so grateful that God has shown me His Grace! Nothing can break me down! I am determined to continue becoming the best version of myself because I owe it to me, my children, and to GOD! I am here to make a difference. I am here to be a shift changer!

I have lived both spectrums of life, abundance and going through hell. I respect both, because in going through all that, I was training to become who I am today! And who I am becoming! Wow! I am rebuilding my life stronger than ever and MY WAY!

I am blessed with an incredible mom, dad and brother. I am beyond blessed with two amazing children who have made me so proud to be their mom. I love you all with all my heart.

I am blessed with wonderful friends who actually have my back. My girl Tricia, wow you have gone through it with me sis and you always were there for me and I'll return the favor. I love you!

God has introduced me to some badass people that I know will join me on this shift changer movement I have in mind. I am building my squad as we speak!

My intention for this year is to be an example to others as I rise up to become the woman that I was intended to be. I intend to excel in my mindset coaching career because I want to imprint the importance of a healthy mindset, body and soul on everyone I can touch. I want to ensure our children will recover from what has happened in these last few years and I want to hold parents, teachers and all of us accountable in doing that! It's a wake up call. Our children need healing, guidance and direction. Let's start by being examples for them.

I want you all to win in life! Let's do this!

The World needs LOVE.

Love begins within ourselves

As a mindset coach, I firmly believe that cultivating self-love is the foundation for experiencing love in all areas of your life. When we truly love ourselves, we become aware of our worth, embrace our uniqueness, and acknowledge our strengths.

Self-love enables us to set healthy boundaries, practice self-care, and prioritize our own well-being. By fostering a positive relationship with ourselves, we open the doors to receiving and giving love abundantly.

Embracing Vulnerability in Love

Love requires vulnerability, and I encourage individuals to embrace it wholeheartedly. Opening ourselves up to love means risking potential hurt and disappointment, but it also offers the opportunity for deep connections and profound joy.

Embracing vulnerability means being authentic, expressing our needs and desires, and allowing ourselves to be seen and heard. It's important to remember that vulnerability is not a weakness, but rather a strength that allows us to experience love in its truest form.

Cultivating a Growth Mindset in Relationships

In the realm of love, a growth mindset is vital for personal and relational growth. I encourage individuals to approach relationships with a willingness to learn, grow, and evolve. This mindset acknowledges that relationships require effort, communication, and a commitment to personal development.

By embracing a growth mindset, we become open to understanding our partners, resolving conflicts, and continuously improving ourselves. With this perspective, setbacks become opportunities for learning, and challenges become catalysts for growth.

Love as a Daily Practice

Love is not just a feeling; it is also an intentional practice. I guide individuals to incorporate love into their daily lives. This practice involves acts of kindness, gratitude, and compassion towards ourselves and others. It means showing up with love, patience, and understanding in our interactions.

Love as a daily practice reminds us to prioritize quality time with loved ones, engage in self-reflection, and cultivate a positive mindset. By making love a conscious choice every day, we create a foundation for fulfilling and meaningful relationships, and an abundant life.

When you struggle in silence.

Heal and then get up and speak your truth.

You need to escape yourself to heal and help others.

Light the world one person at a time.

Order your manifestations like you order Starbucks. What are you looking for in a partner?

Don't start relationships unhealthy,
With addictions,
With attachments,
Looking to fill a void.

Finding someone who makes you feel at home is a wonderful and fulfilling experience. Often times, these connections ignite more of our soul purpose in life. Here are a few suggestions to help you in your search:

1. **Reflect on your values and interests:** Understanding your own values and interests can help you identify someone who aligns with you on a deeper level. Consider the qualities and characteristics that make you feel comfortable and at home.

2. **Expand your social circle:** Engage in activities and join communities that match your interests. This will increase your chances of meeting like-minded individuals who have the potential to make you feel at home.

3. **Be open and authentic:** When interacting with others, be genuine and open about your true self. Authenticity attracts people who appreciate you for who you are and increases the likelihood of finding someone who truly makes you feel comfortable.

4. **Build strong friendships:** Sometimes, a romantic partner may not be the first person to make you feel at home. Close friends can provide a sense of belonging and support. Prioritize cultivating deep, meaningful friendships, as they can lead to connections with individuals who make you feel at home.

5. **Communicate your needs**: Once you've established a connection with someone, it's important to communicate your needs and expectations. Express what makes you feel at home and see if they share similar desires or values. Healthy and open communication is essential for building a strong foundation in any relationship.

6. **Give it time:** Finding someone who makes you feel at home is not an overnight process. It often takes time and multiple connections to find the right person. Be patient and trust that the right individual will come into your life when the timing is right.

Remember, feeling at home with someone goes beyond surface-level compatibility. It involves emotional connection, trust, and shared values. By being true to yourself, engaging in activities you enjoy, and fostering meaningful relationships, you increase your chances of finding that special someone who makes you feel truly at home.

Evolving is an intentional process, but worth it.

When you make an intentional decision to change, you will have to make choices that will break down your ego, pride and the version of yourself that you and others were used to.

As you are rebuilding yourself from the ground up, you will soon realize that you are evolving. With this evolving, of your mind, body and soul, you will begin approaching your life with a growth mindset.

The decision to change becomes a choice and a new way of life. Intentionally choose to evolve!

It's wonderful to hear that you're working on becoming a better version of yourself!

I am proud of you!

As a mindset coach, I can suggest several key areas you can focus on to help you in this journey:

1. **Set clear goals:** Define what you want to achieve and be specific about your objectives. Setting clear goals gives you direction and purpose.

2. **Positive self-talk:** Pay attention to your inner dialogue and replace negative self-talk with positive and empowering statements. Encourage yourself and believe in your abilities.

3. **Embrace self-awareness:** Understand your strengths, weaknesses, values, and beliefs. Self-awareness allows you to make conscious choices aligned with your authentic self.

4. **Cultivate a growth mindset:** Embrace the belief that you can learn, grow, and improve through effort and perseverance. Emphasize progress over perfection and see challenges as opportunities for growth.

5. **Practice gratitude:** Regularly express gratitude for the things you have and the experiences you've had. Gratitude cultivates a positive mindset and helps you appreciate the present moment.

6. **Develop resilience:** Build your ability to bounce back from setbacks and challenges. View failures as learning opportunities and embrace the lessons they offer.

7. **Surround yourself with positive influences:** Seek out supportive and uplifting individuals who inspire you. Engage in communities or groups that align with your goals and values.

8. **Continuous learning:** Embrace a mindset of lifelong learning. Read books, attend seminars, listen to podcasts, or take courses in areas that interest you. Expand your knowledge and skills.

9. **Take care of your well-being:** Prioritize self-care activities such as exercise, proper nutrition, quality sleep, and relaxation techniques. Physical and mental well-being are essential for personal growth.

10. **Practice visualization and affirmations:** Use visualization techniques to imagine yourself achieving your goals. Repeat positive affirmations that reinforce your desired mindset and outcomes.

11. **Take action:** Break down your goals into small, manageable steps, and take consistent action toward them. Progress comes from consistent effort and commitment.

Remember, personal growth is a journey, and it takes time and dedication. Celebrate your progress along the way and be kind to yourself.

You got this!

Recharge Your Mindset.

Recharging your mindset is crucial for overall well-being and personal growth. Just like our bodies need rest and rejuvenation, our minds also require regular recharging to function optimally.

Here are some reasons why recharging your mindset is important.

1. **Mental health:** Taking time to recharge your mindset helps protect and promote good mental health. Our minds can become overwhelmed with stress, negative thoughts, and anxieties. By intentionally engaging in activities that promote relaxation, self-reflection, and positivity, we can alleviate mental strain and enhance our emotional well-being.

2. **Renewed perspective:** When we continuously engage with the same thoughts, routines, and challenges without taking breaks, our perspective can become narrow and stagnant. Recharging your mindset allows you to step back, gain fresh insights, and view situations from different angles. This renewed perspective can lead to innovative solutions, better decision-making, and personal growth.

3. **Increased creativity:** A tired and cluttered mind is less conducive to creativity. When you recharge your mindset, you create space for new ideas to emerge. Engaging in activities such as hobbies, meditation, or spending time in nature can stimulate your imagination, boost creativity, and help you think outside the box.

4. **Enhanced productivity:** Taking regular breaks to recharge your mindset can actually improve your productivity in the long run. When you give yourself time to rest, relax, and rejuvenate, you return to tasks with a refreshed mind and increased focus. This allows you to work more efficiently, make fewer mistakes, and sustain your productivity over time.

5. **Emotional balance:** Recharging your mindset helps you cultivate emotional balance. It allows you to regulate your emotions, manage stress, and build resilience. When you take time to engage in activities that bring you joy, peace, and fulfillment, you develop a stronger emotional foundation that helps you navigate life's challenges with greater ease.

6. **Self-awareness and personal growth:** Recharging your mindset involves self-reflection and introspection. By taking the time to understand your thoughts, emotions, and aspirations, you can gain a deeper understanding of yourself. This self-awareness is essential for personal growth, as it enables you to identify areas for improvement, set meaningful goals, and make positive changes in your life.

In summary, recharging your mindset is vital for your mental health, creativity, productivity, emotional balance, and personal growth. Prioritizing self-care, engaging in activities that bring you joy, and allowing yourself time for rest and reflection are all essential for maintaining a healthy and resilient mindset.

Putting the blame on others is useless.

It's wasted energy that gives life and power to a narrative that is NO longer serving you. Get out of your own way!

The more you feed into that victim mentality, the more you will find that you are nowhere near where you envisioned your life to be.

You can change this!

I encourage you to make peace with all that is dragging you down from the past and start looking at your life as an opportunity to reinvent yourself on a level that you deserve.

It's inside you.

You can do it!

The narrative of the past can be crushed in one statement:

"I will get myself out of anything that is standing in my way."

It's you versus you. Take the setbacks as the fuel needed to evolve and walk into a room and reintroduce yourself.

I was lost to get souled.

I always knew I was chosen for something bigger. When you are hand selected to do something larger than life, the storms are extremely intense, and that's for a reason. That is when you are getting molded to fit into your new role.

Nothing makes sense as it's happening.

However, you find yourself at different stages, being different versions of yourself until you find your soul purpose.

It's magical how it unfolds.

At times, you find yourself in dark places, where you think you can never escape or survive! Those are the times you are evolving into the version of yourself necessary to step into your role as a shift maker.

When you feel it's over and hit rock bottom, and you fear completely losing touch of who you identify with, allow that loss to happen because that is when you find your soul.

Allow the leveling up to occur!

Go back to that inner child, looking into the future and cross the bridge to get to the side where you can impact others on a level you could never imagine.

Surrounding yourself with positive, like-minded people is key, I agree. I challenge you to look at it from a different angle.

Life can be stressful at times. The people around us can add stress to our lives. We have the power to change and/or control that!

Stop the victim mentality and lack mindset today!

Do others bring stress to us, or is it how we perceive, react and respond to someone, or to a situation, that adds stress?

I can guarantee you, if you think back to a situation that occurred in your life and take two, relive it having reacted or responded a different way, you'd realize the stress starts and ends with you. The outcome would have been more positive and less stressful, if you took a step back and saw it differently!

It's how you handle yourself. It's how you look at things. Choose your battles because you're trying to win the war between you, versus you, to become the best you can be. It's that simple!!

Changing your mindset can add years to your life.

Changing your mindset can make you the badass you're meant to be!
Where are you going? How are you going to get there? Are you struggling? It's your mindset that needs to plug in EXACTLY where you want to go, or you're not going anywhere.

I want to spend some time focusing on this subject because, from experience, if you don't prioritize setting specific goals of what you want to achieve, put in the effort and stay consistent, you're going to feel stuck. Your mindset can trap you or it can set you free. You choose!

Here are three suggestions I have to prompt you to realize your mindset is your navigation system and you have to tune into it to maximize your success and to free your mind, to free your life.

1. **Develop a Growth Mindset:** A growth mindset is the belief that your abilities and intelligence can be developed and improved through dedication, effort, and learning. Embrace challenges as opportunities for growth and view failures as learning experiences rather than setbacks. Cultivate a positive and optimistic attitude towards your abilities and potential. By adopting a growth mindset, you'll be more likely to navigate challenges and setbacks effectively, stay motivated, and continuously strive for improvement.

2. **Set Clear and Specific Goals:** To maximize your goals, it's essential to set clear, specific, and measurable objectives. When setting goals, make sure they are aligned with your values and long-term vision. Break down your goals into smaller, manageable steps or milestones. This helps to create a clear roadmap and allows you to track your progress along the way. Additionally, setting realistic deadlines and establishing a system for monitoring and reviewing your goals regularly can help you stay focused and on track.

3. **Practice Positive Self-Talk and Visualization:** The way you speak to yourself and the thoughts you entertain have a significant impact on your mindset. Practice positive self-talk by replacing negative and self-limiting beliefs with empowering and affirming statements. Remind yourself of your strengths, achievements, and past successes to build confidence and self-belief. Visualization is another powerful technique that involves mentally picturing yourself achieving your goals. Imagine the process, the actions you need to take, and the successful outcome. This helps program your mind for success and enhances your motivation and focus.

Remember that mindset is a powerful tool, and it must be supported by consistent action and effort. Utilize these strategies in conjunction with perseverance, discipline, and continuous learning to make the most of your mindset as your navigation system to maximize your goals.

Healing in isolation is necessary.

I am a living testimony of having to go into hermit mode to heal, regroup, reassess and recharge. Let me tell you, it's a shock to your ego when that happens because you have to accept there are layers of yourself that you have to shed to allow a leveling up of your soul to occur. It can get lonely, scary and ugly, BUT, it will amaze you when you find out how resilient and strong you truly are.

We all have light and dark sides of our soul. The light reminds us of who we are and our soul purpose. The dark points out what we have to work on. The choice is yours, whether you want to go through that process, or not. I challenge you to do so! If you choose healing, I can assure you will come out of the process as the diamond you were meant to be!

A life lived without working on healing, in my opinion, is a cop out. You will only be in survival mode. We all have demons we have to face and that's where faith over fear comes in. How sure of yourself are you? How willing are you to do all the work needed, to be able to show up in the world as an example?

Let me give you an example where healing is crucial....

We get licenses to drive, sell real estate and even get married. Right? I believe the license that needs to have the MOST testing is the marriage one. You think because it is time to get married and you love someone, you're ready to commit to being a significant other, and furthermore, have children? Tough love – the answer is NO!

In my opinion, if you haven't done the work to be the best version of yourself, you shouldn't get married and have children because all the issues that weren't dealt with, will bleed into your life and those around you. We all have experienced that to some degree. It's very painful and unpleasant!

Tough stuff to fathom, right?

Do the shadow work. Heal your soul. Deal with your past pains and traumas. Then you can go into the world ready to rock and roll and make that difference.

Life is not a dress rehearsal. "I'm sorry," doesn't heal all actions that hurt deeply! Some hurts can change the trajectory of your life and those you bring into your issues.

Please realize that you can't be of service to others, if you are not willing to accept that it all starts within you.

In order to benefit anyone else, you have to firstly, work on yourself.

A strong #mindset is the new wealth!

Without a strong mindset, programmed to execute words into actions, you're going to hit that DEAD END, over and over again.

I've said it many times, you have to balance your life: mind, body and soul. Take out the trash that occupies space in your head that is needed to succeed. Open up your mind and your life for better!

When you make that peaceful transition, you will think clearly and speak positive life into the words that will embody your every decision, steering you on so many open roads of opportunity.

You want a strong mindset – hire a coach, don't book a trip to get away from your problems and drink them away. How often have you done that? How's that going for you?

You want a stronger body and to tone up and lose weight – hire a trainer. Excuses will not get you to fit into your favorite pair of jeans.

You want to feel grounded and complete, work on your soul – seek spiritual help, pray and meditate.

Are you working on your New Year's Resolutions? I encourage you to work on those daily instead of waiting until the end of the year.

Do it differently, or feel insane doing it the same way and wondering why nothing in your life has changed?

Today is the day you should start!

You'll revive your energy and attain the confidence you need to build the relationships in your life that will be solid and full of purpose.

Find your open road!

Our children are the future.

As a mother of two grown children, I'm very concerned for the future. Things are not moving in the right direction, and if we can't admit it, I'm sure a lot of us see it. We are not on a good path. Things need to shift and change.

How? Integrate mindset strengthening for children, so they can become rockstar adults!

Our minds have the ability to change our lives, in both negative and positive ways. Why aren't we helping our children master this?

I'm asking you to be mindful and let's focus on healing and aiding our children and grandchildren so they can lead fulfilling and functional lives. It starts at home, and should continue throughout their school years.

Raising children nowadays is much more difficult than when I raised mine. I urge parents to pay attention to what their children are doing, feeling and feeding their minds and bodies with. Yes, be that parent. You have to set the standards and examples. Show your children how to live productive and purposeful lives. That's your job! Period. Hold yourselves accountable!

We are obligated as parents, grandparents, uncles and aunts to ensure our children are safe and sound. Focus on what they watch, read and listen to. Feed them nutritious foods to keep them healthy. Show them how prayer and meditation can ground them and ignite their minds, bodies and souls to reach their full potential.

We need to get them out of the stagnant mindset and introduce the growth mindset to them from an early age, so they can lead healthy and successful lives!

www.ingramcontent.com/pod-product-compliance
Lightning Source LLC
LaVergne TN
LVHW060421150225

803718LV00001B/1